I0053063

TEXAS RULES OF EVIDENCE
2019 Edition

Updated through January 1, 2019

Michigan Legal Publishing Ltd.
QUICK DESK REFERENCE SERIES™

Academic and bulk discounts available at
www.michlp.com

WE WELCOME YOUR FEEDBACK: info@michlp.com

ISBN-13: 978-1-64002-053-5

Table of Contents

Article I – General Provisions

Rule 101. Title, Scope, and Applicability of the Rules; Definitions

(a) **Title**. These rules may be cited as the Texas Rules of Evidence.

(b) **Scope**. These rules apply to proceedings in Texas courts except as otherwise provided in subdivisions (d)-(f).

(c) **Rules on Privilege**. The rules on privilege apply to all stages of a case or proceeding.

(d) **Exception for Constitutional or Statutory Provisions or Other Rules**. Despite these rules, a court must admit or exclude evidence if required to do so by the United States or Texas Constitution, a federal or Texas statute, or a rule prescribed by the United States or Texas Supreme Court or the Texas Court of Criminal Appeals. If possible, a court should resolve by reasonable construction any inconsistency between these rules and applicable constitutional or statutory provisions or other rules.

(e) **Exceptions**. These rules-except for those on privilege-do not apply to:

    (1) the court's determination, under Rule 104(a), on a preliminary question of fact governing admissibility;

    (2) grand jury proceedings; and

    (3) the following miscellaneous proceedings:

        (A) an application for habeas corpus in extradition, rendition, or interstate detainer proceedings;

        (B) an inquiry by the court under Code of Criminal Procedure article 46B.004 to determine whether evidence exists that would support a finding that the defendant may be incompetent to stand trial;

        (C) bail proceedings other than hearings to deny, revoke, or increase bail;

        (D) hearings on justification for pretrial detention not involving bail;

        (E) proceedings to issue a search or arrest warrant; and

        (F) direct contempt determination proceedings.

(f) **Exception for Justice Court Cases**. These rules do not apply to justice court cases except as authorized by Texas Rule of Civil Procedure 500.3.

(g) **Exception for Military Justice Hearings**. The Texas Code of Military Justice, Tex. Gov't Code §§ 432.001-432.195, governs the admissibility of evidence in hearings held under that Code.

(h) **Definitions**. In these rules:

(1) "civil case" means a civil action or proceeding;

(2) "criminal case" means a criminal action or proceeding, including an examining trial;

(3) "public office" includes a public agency;

(4) "record" includes a memorandum, report, or data compilation;

(5) a "rule prescribed by the United States or Texas Supreme Court or the Texas Court of Criminal Appeals" means a rule adopted by any of those courts under statutory authority;

(6) "unsworn declaration" means an unsworn declaration made in accordance with Tex. Civ. Prac. & Rem. Code § 132.001; and

(7) a reference to any kind of written material or any other medium includes electronically stored information.

History: Added Feb. 25, 1998, eff. March 1, 1998; amended effective April 1, 2015.

Comment to 2015 Restyling: The reference to "hierarchical governance" in former Rule 101(c) has been deleted as unnecessary. The textual limitation of former Rule 101(c) to criminal cases has been eliminated. Courts in civil cases must also admit or exclude evidence when required to do so by constitutional or statutory provisions or other rules that take precedence over these rules. Likewise, the title to former Rule 101(d) has been changed to more accurately indicate the purpose and scope of the subdivision.

Rule 102. Purpose

These rules should be construed so as to administer every proceeding fairly, eliminate unjustifiable expense and delay, and promote the development of evidence law, to the end of ascertaining the truth and securing a just determination.

History: Added Feb. 25, 1998, eff. March 1, 1998; amended effective April 1, 2015.

Rule 103. Rulings on Evidence

(a) **Preserving a Claim of Error**. A party may claim error in a ruling to admit or exclude evidence only if the error affects a substantial right of the party and:
   (1) if the ruling admits evidence, a party, on the record:
      (A) timely objects or moves to strike; and
      (B) states the specific ground, unless it was apparent from the context; or
   (2) if the ruling excludes evidence, a party informs the court of its substance by an offer of proof, unless the substance was apparent from the context.

(b) **Not Needing to Renew an Objection**. When the court hears a party's objections outside the presence of the jury and rules that evidence is admissible, a party need not renew an objection to preserve a claim of error for appeal.

(c) **Court's Statement About the Ruling; Directing an Offer of Proof**. The court must allow a party to make an offer of proof outside the jury's presence as soon as practicable-and before the court reads its charge to the jury. The court may make any statement about the character or form of the evidence, the objection made, and the ruling. At a party's request, the court must direct that an offer of proof be made in question-and-answer form. Or the court may do so on its own.

(d) **Preventing the Jury from Hearing Inadmissible Evidence**. To the extent practicable, the court must conduct a jury trial so that inadmissible evidence is not suggested to the jury by any means.

(e) **Taking Notice of Fundamental Error in Criminal Cases**. In criminal cases, a court may take notice of a fundamental error affecting a substantial right, even if the claim of error was not properly preserved.

History: Added Feb. 25, 1998, eff. March 1, 1998; amended effective April 1, 2015.

Rule 104. Preliminary Questions

(a) **In General**. The court must decide any preliminary question about whether a witness is qualified, a privilege exists, or evidence is admissible. In so deciding, the court is not bound by evidence rules, except those on privilege.

(b) **Relevance That Depends on a Fact**. When the relevance of evidence depends on whether a fact exists, proof must be introduced sufficient to support a finding that the fact does exist. The court may admit the proposed evidence on the condition that the proof be introduced later.

(c) **Conducting a Hearing So That the Jury Cannot Hear It**. The court must conduct any hearing on a preliminary question so that the jury cannot hear it if:

    (1) the hearing involves the admissibility of a confession in a criminal case;

    (2) a defendant in a criminal case is a witness and so requests; or

    (3) justice so requires.

(d) **Cross-Examining a Defendant in a Criminal Case**. By testifying outside the jury's hearing on a preliminary question, a defendant in a criminal case does not become subject to cross-examination on other issues in the case.

(e) **Evidence Relevant to Weight and Credibility**. This rule does not limit a party's right to introduce before the jury evidence that is relevant to the weight or credibility of other evidence.

History: Added Feb. 25, 1998, eff. March 1, 1998; amended effective April 1, 2015.

Rule 105. Evidence That Is Not Admissible Against Other Parties or for Other Purposes

(a) **Limiting Admitted Evidence**. If the court admits evidence that is admissible against a party or for a purpose-but not against another party or for another purpose-the court, on request, must restrict the evidence to its proper scope and instruct the jury accordingly.

(b) **Preserving a Claim of Error**.

    (1) *Court Admits the Evidence Without Restriction*. A party may claim error in a ruling to admit evidence that is admissible against a party or for a purpose-but not against another party or for another purpose-only if the party requests the court to restrict the evidence to its proper scope and instruct the jury accordingly.

    (2) *Court Excludes the Evidence*. A party may claim error in a ruling to exclude evidence that is admissible against a party or for a purpose-but not against another party or for another

purpose-only if the party limits its offer to the party against whom or the purpose for which the evidence is admissible.

History: Added Feb. 25, 1998, eff. March 1, 1998; amended effective April 1, 2015.

Rule 106. Remainder of or Related Writings or Recorded Statements

If a party introduces all or part of a writing or recorded statement, an adverse party may introduce, at that time, any other part-or any other writing or recorded statement-that in fairness ought to be considered at the same time. "Writing or recorded statement" includes depositions.

History: Added Feb. 25, 1998, eff. March 1, 1998; amended effective April 1, 2015.

Rule 107. Rule of Optional Completeness

If a party introduces part of an act, declaration, conversation, writing, or recorded statement, an adverse party may inquire into any other part on the same subject. An adverse party may also introduce any other act, declaration, conversation, writing, or recorded statement that is necessary to explain or allow the trier of fact to fully understand the part offered by the opponent. "Writing or recorded statement" includes a deposition.

History: Added Feb. 25, 1998, eff. March 1, 1998; amended effective April 1, 2015.

Article II – Judicial Notice

Rule 201. Judicial Notice of Adjudicative Facts

(a) **Scope**. This rule governs judicial notice of an adjudicative fact only, not a legislative fact.
(b) **Kinds of Facts That May Be Judicially Noticed**. The court may judicially notice a fact that is not subject to reasonable dispute because it:
    (1) is generally known within the trial court's territorial jurisdiction; or

    (2) can be accurately and readily determined from sources whose accuracy cannot reasonably be questioned.
(c) **Taking Notice**. The court:
    (1) may take judicial notice on its own; or
    (2) must take judicial notice if a party requests it and the court is supplied with the necessary information.
(d) **Timing**. The court may take judicial notice at any stage of the proceeding.
(e) **Opportunity to Be Heard**. On timely request, a party is entitled to be heard on the propriety of taking judicial notice and the nature of the fact to be noticed. If the court takes judicial notice before notifying a party, the party, on request, is still entitled to be heard.
(f) **Instructing the Jury**. In a civil case, the court must instruct the jury to accept the noticed fact as conclusive. In a criminal case, the court must instruct the jury that it may or may not accept the noticed fact as conclusive.

History: Added Feb. 25, 1998, eff. March 1, 1998; amended effective April 1, 2015.

Rule 202. Judicial Notice of Other States' Law

(a) **Scope**. This rule governs judicial notice of another state's, territory's, or federal jurisdiction's:
- Constitution;
- public statutes;
- rules;
- regulations;
- ordinances;
- court decisions; and
- common law.
(b) **Taking Notice**. The court:
    (1) may take judicial notice on its own; or
    (2) must take judicial notice if a party requests it and the court is supplied with the necessary information.
(c) **Notice and Opportunity to Be Heard**.
    (1) *Notice*. The court may require a party requesting judicial notice to notify all other parties of the request so they may respond to it.

(2) *Opportunity to Be Heard*. On timely request, a party is entitled to be heard on the propriety of taking judicial notice and the nature of the matter to be noticed. If the court takes judicial notice before a party has been notified, the party, on request, is still entitled to be heard.

(d) **Timing**. The court may take judicial notice at any stage of the proceeding.

(e) **Determination and Review**. The court-not the jury-must determine the law of another state, territory, or federal jurisdiction. The court's determination must be treated as a ruling on a question of law.

History: Added Feb. 25, 1998, eff. March 1, 1998; amended effective April 1, 2015.

Rule 203. Determining Foreign Law

(a) **Raising a Foreign Law Issue**. A party who intends to raise an issue about a foreign country's law must:
   (1) give reasonable notice by a pleading or other writing; and
   (2) at least 30 days before trial, supply all parties a copy of any written materials or sources the party intends to use to prove the foreign law.

(b) **Translations**. If the materials or sources were originally written in a language other than English, the party intending to rely on them must, at least 30 days before trial, supply all parties both a copy of the foreign language text and an English translation.

(c) **Materials the Court May Consider; Notice**. In determining foreign law, the court may consider any material or source, whether or not admissible. If the court considers any material or source not submitted by a party, it must give all parties notice and a reasonable opportunity to comment and submit additional materials.

(d) **Determination and Review**. The court-not the jury-must determine foreign law. The court's determination must be treated as a ruling on a question of law.

(e) **Suits Brought Under the Family Code Involving a Marriage Relationship or Parent-Child Relationship**. Subsections (a) and (b) of this rule do not apply to an action to which Rule 308b, Texas Rules of Civil Procedure, apply.

History: Added Feb. 25, 1998, eff. March 1, 1998; amended effective April 1, 2015; amended effective January 1, 2018.

Rule 204. Judicial Notice of Texas Municipal and County Ordinances, Texas Register Contents, and Published Agency Rules

(a) **Scope**. This rule governs judicial notice of Texas municipal and county ordinances, the contents of the Texas Register, and agency rules published in the Texas Administrative Code.

(b) **Taking Notice**. The court:
   (1) may take judicial notice on its own; or
   (2) must take judicial notice if a party requests it and the court is supplied with the necessary information.

(c) **Notice and Opportunity to Be Heard**.
   (1) *Notice*. The court may require a party requesting judicial notice to notify all other parties of the request so they may respond to it.
   (2) *Opportunity to Be Heard*. On timely request, a party is entitled to be heard on the propriety of taking judicial notice and the nature of the matter to be noticed. If the court takes judicial notice before a party has been notified, the party, on request, is still entitled to be heard.

(d) **Determination and Review**. The court-not the jury-must determine municipal and county ordinances, the contents of the Texas Register, and published agency rules. The court's determination must be treated as a ruling on a question of law.

History: Added Feb. 25, 1998, eff. March 1, 1998; amended effective April 1, 2015.

Article III – Presumptions

[No rules adopted at this time.]

Article IV – Relevance and its Limits

Rule 401. Test for Relevant Evidence

Evidence is relevant if:

(a) it has any tendency to make a fact more or less probable than it would be without the evidence; and

(b) the fact is of consequence in determining the action.

History: Added Feb. 25, 1998, eff. March 1, 1998; amended effective April 1, 2015.

Rule 402. Relevant Evidence Generally Admissible; Irrelevant Evidence Inadmissible

Relevant evidence is admissible unless any of the following provides otherwise:

- the United States or Texas Constitution;
- a statute;
- these rules; or
- other rules prescribed under statutory authority.

Irrelevant evidence is not admissible.

History: Added Feb. 25, 1998, eff. March 1, 1998; amended effective April 1, 2015.

Rule 403. Excluding Relevant Evidence for Prejudice, Confusion, or Other Reasons

The court may exclude relevant evidence if its probative value is substantially outweighed by a danger of one or more of the following: unfair prejudice, confusing the issues, misleading the jury, undue delay, or needlessly presenting cumulative evidence.

History: Added Feb. 25, 1998, eff. March 1, 1998; amended effective April 1, 2015.

Rule 404. Character Evidence; Crimes or Other Acts

(a) **Character Evidence**.
  (1) *Prohibited Uses*. Evidence of a person's character or character trait is not admissible to prove that on a particular occasion the person acted in accordance with the character or trait.
  (2) *Exceptions for an Accused*.
    (A) In a criminal case, a defendant may offer evidence of the defendant's pertinent trait, and if the evidence is admitted, the prosecutor may offer evidence to rebut it.
    (B) In a civil case, a party accused of conduct involving moral turpitude may offer evidence of the party's pertinent trait,

and if the evidence is admitted, the accusing party may offer evidence to rebut it.

(3) *Exceptions for a Victim*.

   (A) In a criminal case, subject to the limitations in Rule 412, a defendant may offer evidence of a victim's pertinent trait, and if the evidence is admitted, the prosecutor may offer evidence to rebut it.

   (B) In a homicide case, the prosecutor may offer evidence of the victim's trait of peacefulness to rebut evidence that the victim was the first aggressor.

   (C) In a civil case, a party accused of assaultive conduct may offer evidence of the victim's trait of violence to prove self-defense, and if the evidence is admitted, the accusing party may offer evidence of the victim's trait of peacefulness.

(4) *Exceptions for a Witness*. Evidence of a witness's character may be admitted under Rules 607, 608, and 609.

(5) *Definition of "Victim."* In this rule, "victim" includes an alleged victim.

(b) **Crimes, Wrongs, or Other Acts**.

(1) *Prohibited Uses*. Evidence of a crime, wrong, or other act is not admissible to prove a person's character in order to show that on a particular occasion the person acted in accordance with the character.

(2) *Permitted Uses; Notice in Criminal Case*. This evidence may be admissible for another purpose, such as proving motive, opportunity, intent, preparation, plan, knowledge, identity, absence of mistake, or lack of accident. On timely request by a defendant in a criminal case, the prosecutor must provide reasonable notice before trial that the prosecution intends to introduce such evidence-other than that arising in the same transaction-in its case-in-chief.

History: Added Feb. 25, 1998, eff. March 1, 1998; amended effective April 1, 2015.

Rule 405. Methods of Proving Character

(a) **By Reputation or Opinion**.

(1) *In General*. When evidence of a person's character or character trait is admissible, it may be proved by testimony about the person's reputation or by testimony in the form of an opinion.

On cross-examination of the character witness, inquiry may be made into relevant specific instances of the person's conduct.

(2) *Accused's Character in a Criminal Case*. In the guilt stage of a criminal case, a witness may testify to the defendant's character or character trait only if, before the day of the offense, the witness was familiar with the defendant's reputation or the facts or information that form the basis of the witness's opinion.

(b) **By Specific Instances of Conduct**. When a person's character or character trait is an essential element of a charge, claim, or defense, the character or trait may also be proved by relevant specific instances of the person's conduct.

History: Added Feb. 25, 1998, eff. March 1, 1998; amended effective April 1, 2015.

Rule 406. Habit; Routine Practice

Evidence of a person's habit or an organization's routine practice may be admitted to prove that on a particular occasion the person or organization acted in accordance with the habit or routine practice. The court may admit this evidence regardless of whether it is corroborated or whether there was an eyewitness.

History: Added Feb. 25, 1998, eff. March 1, 1998; amended effective April 1, 2015.

Rule 407. Subsequent Remedial Measures; Notification of Defect

(a) **Subsequent Remedial Measures**. When measures are taken that would have made an earlier injury or harm less likely to occur, evidence of the subsequent measures is not admissible to prove:
- negligence;
- culpable conduct;
- a defect in a product or its design; or
- a need for a warning or instruction.

But the court may admit this evidence for another purpose, such as impeachment or-if disputed-proving ownership, control, or the feasibility of precautionary measures.

(b) **Notification of Defect**. A manufacturer's written notification to a purchaser of a defect in one of its products is admissible against the manufacturer to prove the defect.

History: Added Feb. 25, 1998, eff. March 1, 1998; amended effective April 1, 2015.

Comment to 2015 Restyling: Rule 407 previously provided that evidence was not excluded if offered for a purpose not explicitly prohibited by the Rule. To improve the language of the Rule, it now provides that the court may admit evidence if offered for a permissible purpose. There is no intent to change the process for admitting evidence covered by the Rule. It remains the case that if offered for an impermissible purpose, it must be excluded, and if offered for a purpose not barred by the Rule, its admissibility remains governed by the general principles of Rules 402, 403, 801, etc.

Rule 408. Compromise Offers and Negotiations

(a) **Prohibited Uses**. Evidence of the following is not admissible either to prove or disprove the validity or amount of a disputed claim:
   (1) furnishing, promising, or offering-or accepting, promising to accept, or offering to accept-a valuable consideration in compromising or attempting to compromise the claim; and
   (2) conduct or statements made during compromise negotiations about the claim.
(b) **Permissible Uses**. The court may admit this evidence for another purpose, such as proving a party's or witness's bias, prejudice, or interest, negating a contention of undue delay, or proving an effort to obstruct a criminal investigation or prosecution.

History: Added Feb. 25, 1998, eff. March 1, 1998; amended effective April 1, 2015.

Comment to 2015 Restyling: Rule 408 previously provided that evidence was not excluded if offered for a purpose not explicitly prohibited by the Rule. To improve the language of the Rule, it now provides that the court may admit evidence if offered for a permissible purpose. There is no intent to change the process for admitting evidence covered by the Rule. It remains the case that if offered for an impermissible purpose, it must be excluded, and if offered for a purpose not barred by the Rule, its admissibility remains governed by the general principles of Rules 402, 403, 801, etc.

The reference to "liability" has been deleted on the ground that the deletion makes the Rule flow better and easier to read, and because "liability" is covered by the broader term "validity." Courts have not made substantive decisions on the basis of any distinction between validity and liability. No change in current practice or in the coverage of the Rule is intended.

Finally, the sentence of the Rule referring to evidence "otherwise discoverable" has been deleted as superfluous. The intent of the sentence was to prevent a party from trying to immunize admissible information, such as a pre-existing document, through the pretense of disclosing it during compromise negotiations. But even without the sentence, the Rule cannot be read to protect pre-existing information simply because it was presented to the adversary in compromise negotiations.

Rule 409. Offers to Pay Medical and Similar Expenses

Evidence of furnishing, promising to pay, or offering to pay medical, hospital, or similar expenses resulting from an injury is not admissible to prove liability for the injury.

History: Added Feb. 25, 1998, eff. March 1, 1998; amended effective April 1, 2015.

Rule 410. Pleas, Plea Discussions and Related Statements

(a) **Prohibited Uses in Civil Cases**. In a civil case, evidence of the following is not admissible against the defendant who made the plea or was a participant in the plea discussions:
  (1) a guilty plea that was later withdrawn;
  (2) a nolo contendere plea;
  (3) a statement made during a proceeding on either of those pleas under Federal Rule of Criminal Procedure 11 or a comparable state procedure; or
  (4) a statement made during plea discussions with an attorney for the prosecuting authority if the discussions did not result in a guilty plea or they resulted in a later-withdrawn guilty plea.

(b) **Prohibited Uses in Criminal Cases**. In a criminal case, evidence of the following is not admissible against the defendant who made the plea or was a participant in the plea discussions:

(1) a guilty plea that was later withdrawn;

(2) a nolo contendere plea that was later withdrawn;

(3) a statement made during a proceeding on either of those pleas under Federal Rule of Criminal Procedure 11 or a comparable state procedure; or

(4) a statement made during plea discussions with an attorney for the prosecuting authority if the discussions did not result in a guilty or nolo contendere plea or they resulted in a later-withdrawn guilty or nolo contendere plea.

(c) **Exception**. In a civil case, the court may admit a statement described in paragraph (a)(3) or (4) and in a criminal case, the court may admit a statement described in paragraph (b)(3) or (4), when another statement made during the same plea or plea discussions has been introduced and in fairness the statements ought to be considered together.

History: Added Feb. 25, 1998, eff. March 1, 1998; amended effective April 1, 2015.

Rule 411. Liability Insurance

Evidence that a person was or was not insured against liability is not admissible to prove whether the person acted negligently or otherwise wrongfully. But the court may admit this evidence for another purpose, such as proving a witness's bias or prejudice or, if disputed, proving agency, ownership, or control.

History: Added Feb. 25, 1998, eff. March 1, 1998; amended effective April 1, 2015.

Rule 412. Evidence of Previous Sexual Conduct in Criminal Cases

(a) **In General**. The following evidence is not admissible in a prosecution for sexual assault, aggravated sexual assault, or attempt to commit sexual assault or aggravated sexual assault: (1) reputation or opinion evidence of a victim's past sexual behavior; or (2) specific instances of a victim's past sexual behavior.

(b) **Exceptions for Specific Instances**. Evidence of specific instances of a victim's past sexual behavior is admissible if:

(1) the court admits the evidence in accordance with subdivisions (c) and (d);

(2) the evidence:

(A) is necessary to rebut or explain scientific or medical evidence offered by the prosecutor;

(B) concerns past sexual behavior with the defendant and is offered by the defendant to prove consent;

(C) relates to the victim's motive or bias;

(D) is admissible under Rule 609; or

(E) is constitutionally required to be admitted; and

(3) the probative value of the evidence outweighs the danger of unfair prejudice.

(c) **Procedure for Offering Evidence**. Before offering any evidence of the victim's past sexual behavior, the defendant must inform the court outside the jury's presence. The court must then conduct an in camera hearing, recorded by a court reporter, and determine whether the proposed evidence is admissible. The defendant may not refer to any evidence ruled inadmissible without first requesting and gaining the court's approval outside the jury's presence.

(d) **Record Sealed**. The court must preserve the record of the in camera hearing, under seal, as part of the record.

(e) **Definition of "Victim."** In this rule, "victim" includes an alleged victim.

History: Added Feb. 25, 1998, eff. March 1, 1998; amended effective January 1, 2007; amended effective April 1, 2015.

Article V – Privileges

Rule 501. Privileges in General

Unless a Constitution, a statute, or these or other rules prescribed under statutory authority provide otherwise, no person has a privilege to:

(a) refuse to be a witness;

(b) refuse to disclose any matter;

(c) refuse to produce any object or writing; or

(d) prevent another from being a witness, disclosing any matter, or producing any object or writing.

History: Added Feb. 25, 1998, eff. March 1, 1998; amended effective April 1, 2015.

Rule 502. Required Reports Privileged by Statute

(a) **In General**. If a law requiring a return or report to be made so provides:
   (1) a person, corporation, association, or other organization or entity-whether public or private-that makes the required return or report has a privilege to refuse to disclose it and to prevent any other person from disclosing it; and
   (2) a public officer or agency to whom the return or report must be made has a privilege to refuse to disclose it.
(b) **Exceptions**. This privilege does not apply in an action involving perjury, false statements, fraud in the return or report, or other failure to comply with the law in question.

History: Added Feb. 25, 1998, eff. March 1, 1998; amended effective April 1, 2015.

Rule 503. Lawyer-Client Privilege

(a) **Definitions**. In this rule:
   (1) A "client" is a person, public officer, or corporation, association, or other organization or entity-whether public or private-that:
     (A) is rendered professional legal services by a lawyer; or
     (B) consults a lawyer with a view to obtaining professional legal services from the lawyer.
   (2) A "client's representative" is:
     (A) a person who has authority to obtain professional legal services for the client or to act for the client on the legal advice rendered; or
     (B) any other person who, to facilitate the rendition of professional legal services to the client, makes or receives a confidential communication while acting in the scope of employment for the client.
   (3) A "lawyer" is a person authorized, or who the client reasonably believes is authorized, to practice law in any state or nation.
   (4) A "lawyer's representative" is:
     (A) one employed by the lawyer to assist in the rendition of professional legal services; or

     (B) an accountant who is reasonably necessary for the lawyer's rendition of professional legal services.

    (5) A communication is "confidential" if not intended to be disclosed to third persons other than those:

     (A) to whom disclosure is made to further the rendition of professional legal services to the client; or

     (B) reasonably necessary to transmit the communication.

(b) **Rules of Privilege**.

    (1) General Rule. A client has a privilege to refuse to disclose and to prevent any other person from disclosing confidential communications made to facilitate the rendition of professional legal services to the client:

     (A) between the client or the client's representative and the client's lawyer or the lawyer's representative;

     (B) between the client's lawyer and the lawyer's representative;

     (C) by the client, the client's representative, the client's lawyer, or the lawyer's representative to a lawyer representing another party in a pending action or that lawyer's representative, if the communications concern a matter of common interest in the pending action;

     (D) between the client's representatives or between the client and the client's representative; or

     (E) among lawyers and their representatives representing the same client.

    (2) Special Rule in a Criminal Case. In a criminal case, a client has a privilege to prevent a lawyer or lawyer's representative from disclosing any other fact that came to the knowledge of the lawyer or the lawyer's representative by reason of the attorney-client relationship.

(c) **Who May Claim**. The privilege may be claimed by:

    (1) the client;

    (2) the client's guardian or conservator;

    (3) a deceased client's personal representative; or

    (4) the successor, trustee, or similar representative of a corporation, association, or other organization or entity-whether or not in existence.

The person who was the client's lawyer or the lawyer's representative when the communication was made may claim the privilege on the client's behalf-and is presumed to have authority to do so.

(d) **Exceptions**. This privilege does not apply:
  (1) Furtherance of Crime or Fraud. If the lawyer's services were sought or obtained to enable or aid anyone to commit or plan to commit what the client knew or reasonably should have known to be a crime or fraud.
  (2) Claimants Through Same Deceased Client. If the communication is relevant to an issue between parties claiming through the same deceased client.
  (3) Breach of Duty By a Lawyer or Client. If the communication is relevant to an issue of breach of duty by a lawyer to the client or by a client to the lawyer.
  (4) Document Attested By a Lawyer. If the communication is relevant to an issue concerning an attested document to which the lawyer is an attesting witness.
  (5) Joint Clients. If the communication:
    (A) is offered in an action between clients who retained or consulted a lawyer in common;
    (B) was made by any of the clients to the lawyer; and
    (C) is relevant to a matter of common interest between the clients.

History: Added Feb. 25, 1998, eff. March 1, 1998; amended effective April 1, 2015.

Rule 504. Spousal Privileges

(a) **Confidential Communication Privilege**.
  (1) *Definition*. A communication is "confidential" if a person makes it privately to the person's spouse and does not intend its disclosure to any other person.
  (2) *General Rule*. A person has a privilege to refuse to disclose and to prevent any other person from disclosing a confidential communication made to the person's spouse while they were married. This privilege survives termination of the marriage.
  (3) *Who May Claim*. The privilege may be claimed by:
    (A) the communicating spouse;
    (B) the guardian of a communicating spouse who is incompetent; or
    (C) the personal representative of a communicating spouse who is deceased. The other spouse may claim the privilege on

the communicating spouse's behalf-and is presumed to
have authority to do so.

(4) *Exceptions.* This privilege does not apply:

    (A) Furtherance of Crime or Fraud. If the communication is
made-wholly or partially-to enable or aid anyone to commit
or plan to commit a crime or fraud.

    (B) Proceeding Between Spouse and Other Spouse or Claimant
Through Deceased Spouse. In a civil proceeding:

        (i) brought by or on behalf of one spouse against the
other; or

        (ii) between a surviving spouse and a person claiming
through the deceased spouse.

    (C) Crime Against Family, Spouse, Household Member, or
Minor Child. In a:

        (i) proceeding in which a party is accused of conduct that,
if proved, is a crime against the person of the other
spouse, any member of the household of either spouse,
or any minor child; or

        (ii) criminal proceeding involving a charge of bigamy
under Section 25.01 of the Penal Code.

    (D) Commitment or Similar Proceeding. In a proceeding to
commit either spouse or otherwise to place the spouse or
the spouse's property under another's control because of a
mental or physical condition.

    (E) Proceeding to Establish Competence. In a proceeding
brought by or on behalf of either spouse to establish
competence.

(b) **Privilege Not to Testify in a Criminal Case**.

(1) *General Rule.* In a criminal case, an accused's spouse has a
privilege not to be called to testify for the state. But this rule
neither prohibits a spouse from testifying voluntarily for the
state nor gives a spouse a privilege to refuse to be called to
testify for the accused.

(2) *Failure to Call Spouse.* If other evidence indicates that the
accused's spouse could testify to relevant matters, an accused's
failure to call the spouse to testify is a proper subject of
comment by counsel.

(3) *Who May Claim.* The privilege not to testify may be claimed by
the accused's spouse or the spouse's guardian or representative,
but not by the accused.

(4) *Exceptions*. This privilege does not apply:
   (A) Certain Criminal Proceedings. In a criminal proceeding in which a spouse is charged with:
      (i) a crime against the other spouse, any member of the household of either spouse, or any minor child; or
      (ii) bigamy under Section 25.01 of the Penal Code.
   (B) Matters That Occurred Before the Marriage. If the spouse is called to testify about matters that occurred before the marriage.

History: Added Feb. 25, 1998, eff. March 1, 1998; amended effective January 1, 2007; amended effective April 1, 2015.

Comment to 2015 Restyling: Previously, Rule 504(b)(1) provided that, "A spouse who testifies on behalf of an accused is subject to cross-examination as provided in Rule 611(b)." That sentence was included in the original version of Rule 504 when the Texas Rules of Criminal Evidence were promulgated in 1986 and changed the rule to a testimonial privilege held by the witness spouse. Until then, a spouse was deemed incompetent to testify against his or her defendant spouse, and when a spouse testified on behalf of a defendant spouse, the state was limited to cross-examining the spouse about matters relating to the spouse's direct testimony. The quoted sentence from the original Criminal Rule 504(b) was designed to overturn this limitation and allow the state to cross-examine a testifying spouse in the same manner as any other witness. More than twenty-five years later, it is clear that a spouse who testifies either for or against a defendant spouse may be cross-examined in the same manner as any other witness. Therefore, the continued inclusion in the rule of a provision that refers only to the cross-examination of a spouse who testifies on behalf of the accused is more confusing than helpful. Its deletion is designed to clarify the rule and does not change existing law.

Rule 505. Privilege for Communications to a Clergy Member

(a) **Definitions**. In this rule:
   (1) A "clergy member" is a minister, priest, rabbi, accredited Christian Science Practitioner, or other similar functionary of a religious organization or someone whom a communicant reasonably believes is a clergy member.

(2) A "communicant" is a person who consults a clergy member in the clergy member's professional capacity as a spiritual adviser.

(3) A communication is "confidential" if made privately and not intended for further disclosure except to other persons present to further the purpose of the communication.

(b) **General Rule**. A communicant has a privilege to refuse to disclose and to prevent any other person from disclosing a confidential communication by the communicant to a clergy member in the clergy member's professional capacity as spiritual adviser.

(c) **Who May Claim**. The privilege may be claimed by:

(1) the communicant;

(2) the communicant's guardian or conservator; or

(3) a deceased communicant's personal representative.

The clergy member to whom the communication was made may claim the privilege on the communicant's behalf-and is presumed to have authority to do so.

History: Added Feb. 25, 1998, eff. March 1, 1998; amended effective April 1, 2015.

Rule 506. Political Vote Privilege

A person has a privilege to refuse to disclose the person's vote at a political election conducted by secret ballot unless the vote was cast illegally.

History: Added Feb. 25, 1998, eff. March 1, 1998; amended effective April 1, 2015.

Rule 507. Trade Secrets Privilege

(a) **General Rule**. A person has a privilege to refuse to disclose and to prevent other persons from disclosing a trade secret owned by the person, unless the court finds that nondisclosure will tend to conceal fraud or otherwise work injustice.

(b) **Who May Claim**. The privilege may be claimed by the person who owns the trade secret or the person's agent or employee.

(c) **Protective Measure**. If a court orders a person to disclose a trade secret, it must take any protective measure required by the interests of the privilege holder and the parties and to further justice.

History: Added Feb. 25, 1998, eff. March 1, 1998; amended effective April 1, 2015.

Rule 508. Informer's Identity Privilege

(a) **General Rule**. The United States, a state, or a subdivision of either has a privilege to refuse to disclose a person's identity if:

    (1) the person has furnished information to a law enforcement officer or a member of a legislative committee or its staff conducting an investigation of a possible violation of law; and

    (2) the information relates to or assists in the investigation.

(b) **Who May Claim**. The privilege may be claimed by an appropriate representative of the public entity to which the informer furnished the information. The court in a criminal case must reject the privilege claim if the state objects.

(c) **Exceptions**.

    (1) *Voluntary Disclosure; Informer a Witness*. This privilege does not apply if:

        (A) the informer's identity or the informer's interest in the communication's subject matter has been disclosed-by a privilege holder or the informer's own action-to a person who would have cause to resent the communication; or

        (B) the informer appears as a witness for the public entity.

    (2) *Testimony About the Merits*.

        (A) Criminal Case. In a criminal case, this privilege does not apply if the court finds a reasonable probability exists that the informer can give testimony necessary to a fair determination of guilt or innocence. If the court so finds and the public entity elects not to disclose the informer's identity:

            (i) on the defendant's motion, the court must dismiss the charges to which the testimony would relate; or

            (ii) on its own motion, the court may dismiss the charges to which the testimony would relate.

        (B) Certain Civil Cases. In a civil case in which the public entity is a party, this privilege does not apply if the court finds a reasonable probability exists that the informer can give testimony necessary to a fair determination of a material issue on the merits. If the court so finds and the public entity elects not to disclose the informer's identity, the court may make any order that justice requires.

(C) Procedures.

   (i) If it appears that an informer may be able to give the testimony required to invoke this exception and the public entity claims the privilege, the court must give the public entity an opportunity to show in camera facts relevant to determining whether this exception is met. The showing should ordinarily be made by affidavits, but the court may take testimony if it finds the matter cannot be satisfactorily resolved by affidavits.

   (ii) No counsel or party may attend the in camera showing.

   (iii) The court must seal and preserve for appeal evidence submitted under this subparagraph (2)(C). The evidence must not otherwise be revealed without the public entity's consent.

(3) *Legality of Obtaining Evidence*.

   (A) Court May Order Disclosure. The court may order the public entity to disclose an informer's identity if:

      (i) information from an informer is relied on to establish the legality of the means by which evidence was obtained; and

      (ii) the court is not satisfied that the information was received from an informer reasonably believed to be reliable or credible.

   (B) Procedures.

      (i) On the public entity's request, the court must order the disclosure be made in camera.

      (ii) No counsel or party may attend the in camera disclosure.

      (iii) If the informer's identity is disclosed in camera, the court must seal and preserve for appeal the record of the in camera proceeding. The record of the in camera proceeding must not otherwise be revealed without the public entity's consent.

History: Added Feb. 25, 1998, eff. March 1, 1998; amended effective April 1, 2015.

Rule 509. Physician-Patient Privilege

(a) **Definitions**. In this rule:

(1) A "patient" is a person who consults or is seen by a physician for medical care.

(2) A "physician" is a person licensed, or who the patient reasonably believes is licensed, to practice medicine in any state or nation.

(3) A communication is "confidential" if not intended to be disclosed to third persons other than those:

    (A) present to further the patient's interest in the consultation, examination, or interview;

    (B) reasonably necessary to transmit the communication; or

    (C) participating in the diagnosis and treatment under the physician's direction, including members of the patient's family.

(b) **Limited Privilege in a Criminal Case**. There is no physician-patient privilege in a criminal case. But a confidential communication is not admissible in a criminal case if made:

(1) to a person involved in the treatment of or examination for alcohol or drug abuse; and

(2) by a person being treated voluntarily or being examined for admission to treatment for alcohol or drug abuse.

(c) **General Rule in a Civil Case**. In a civil case, a patient has a privilege to refuse to disclose and to prevent any other person from disclosing:

(1) a confidential communication between a physician and the patient that relates to or was made in connection with any professional services the physician rendered the patient; and

(2) a record of the patient's identity, diagnosis, evaluation, or treatment created or maintained by a physician.

(d) **Who May Claim in a Civil Case**. The privilege may be claimed by:

(1) the patient; or

(2) the patient's representative on the patient's behalf.

The physician may claim the privilege on the patient's behalf-and is presumed to have authority to do so.

(e) **Exceptions in a Civil Case**. This privilege does not apply:

(1) *Proceeding Against Physician*. If the communication or record is relevant to a claim or defense in:

    (A) a proceeding the patient brings against a physician; or

    (B) a license revocation proceeding in which the patient is a complaining witness.

(2) *Consent.* If the patient or a person authorized to act on the patient's behalf consents in writing to the release of any privileged information, as provided in subdivision (f).

(3) *Action to Collect.* In an action to collect a claim for medical services rendered to the patient.

(4) *Party Relies on Patient's Condition.* If any party relies on the patient's physical, mental, or emotional condition as a part of the party's claim or defense and the communication or record is relevant to that condition.

(5) *Disciplinary Investigation or Proceeding.* In a disciplinary investigation of or proceeding against a physician under the Medical Practice Act, Tex. Occ. Code § 164.001 et seq., or a registered nurse under Tex. Occ. Code § 301.451 et seq. But the board conducting the investigation or proceeding must protect the identity of any patient whose medical records are examined unless:
   (A) the patient's records would be subject to disclosure under paragraph (e)(1); or
   (B) the patient has consented in writing to the release of medical records, as provided in subdivision (f).

(6) *Involuntary Civil Commitment or Similar Proceeding.* In a proceeding for involuntary civil commitment or court-ordered treatment, or a probable cause hearing under Tex. Health & Safety Code:
   (A) chapter 462 (Treatment of Persons With Chemical Dependencies);
   (B) title 7, subtitle C (Texas Mental Health Code); or
   (C) title 7, subtitle D (Persons With an Intellectual Disability Act).

(7) *Abuse or Neglect of "Institution" Resident.* In a proceeding regarding the abuse or neglect, or the cause of any abuse or neglect, of a resident of an "institution" as defined in Tex. Health & Safety Code § 242.002.

(f) **Consent For Release of Privileged Information**.
   (1) Consent for the release of privileged information must be in writing and signed by:
   (A) the patient;
   (B) a parent or legal guardian if the patient is a minor;
   (C) a legal guardian if the patient has been adjudicated incompetent to manage personal affairs;

(D) an attorney appointed for the patient under Tex. Health & Safety Code title 7, subtitles C and D;

(E) an attorney ad litem appointed for the patient under Tex. Estates Code title 3, subtitle C;

(F) an attorney ad litem or guardian ad litem appointed for a minor under Tex. Fam. Code chapter 107, subchapter B; or

(G) a personal representative if the patient is deceased.

(2) The consent must specify:

(A) the information or medical records covered by the release;

(B) the reasons or purposes for the release; and

(C) the person to whom the information is to be released.

(3) The patient, or other person authorized to consent, may withdraw consent to the release of any information. But a withdrawal of consent does not affect any information disclosed before the patient or authorized person gave written notice of the withdrawal.

(4) Any person who receives information privileged under this rule may disclose the information only to the extent consistent with the purposes specified in the consent.

History: Added Feb. 25, 1998, eff. March 1, 1998; amended effective April 1, 2015.

Comment to 2015 Restyling: The physician-patient privilege in a civil case was first enacted in Texas in 1981 as part of the Medical Practice Act, formerly codified in Tex. Rev. Civ. Stat. art. 4495b. That statute provided that the privilege applied even if a patient had received a physician's services before the statute's enactment. Because more than thirty years have now passed, it is no longer necessary to burden the text of the rule with a statement regarding the privilege's retroactive application. But deleting this statement from the rule's text is not intended as a substantive change in the law.

The former rule's reference to "confidentiality or" and "administrative proceedings" in subdivision (e) [Exceptions in a Civil Case] has been deleted. First, this rule is a privilege rule only. Tex. Occ. Code § 159.004 sets forth exceptions to a physician's duty to maintain confidentiality of patient information outside court and administrative proceedings. Second, by their own terms the rules of evidence govern only proceedings in Texas courts. See Rule 101(b). To the extent the rules apply in administrative proceedings, it is because the Administrative Procedure Act mandates their applicability. Tex. Gov't Code § 2001.083 provides that "[i]n a contested case, a state agency shall give effect to the rules of privilege recognized by law." Section 2001.091 excludes privileged material from discovery in contested administrative cases.

Statutory references in the former rule that are no longer up-to-date have been revised. Finally, reconciling the provisions of Rule 509 with the parts of Tex. Occ. Code ch. 159 that address a physician-patient privilege applicable to court proceedings is beyond the scope of the restyling project.

Rule 510. Mental Health Information Privilege in Civil Cases

(a) **Definitions**. In this rule:
    (1) A "professional" is a person:
        (A) authorized to practice medicine in any state or nation;
        (B) licensed or certified by the State of Texas in the diagnosis, evaluation, or treatment of any mental or emotional disorder;
        (C) involved in the treatment or examination of drug abusers; or
        (D) who the patient reasonably believes to be a professional under this rule.
    (2) A "patient" is a person who:
        (A) consults or is interviewed by a professional for diagnosis, evaluation, or treatment of any mental or emotional condition or disorder, including alcoholism and drug addiction; or
        (B) is being treated voluntarily or being examined for admission to voluntary treatment for drug abuse.
    (3) A "patient's representative" is:
        (A) any person who has the patient's written consent;
        (B) the parent of a minor patient;
        (C) the guardian of a patient who has been adjudicated incompetent to manage personal affairs; or
        (D) the personal representative of a deceased patient.
    (4) A communication is "confidential" if not intended to be disclosed to third persons other than those:
        (A) present to further the patient's interest in the diagnosis, examination, evaluation, or treatment;

      (B) reasonably necessary to transmit the communication; or

      (C) participating in the diagnosis, examination, evaluation, or treatment under the professional's direction, including members of the patient's family.

(b) **General Rule; Disclosure**.

    (1) In a civil case, a patient has a privilege to refuse to disclose and to prevent any other person from disclosing:

      (A) a confidential communication between the patient and a professional; and

      (B) a record of the patient's identity, diagnosis, evaluation, or treatment that is created or maintained by a professional.

    (2) In a civil case, any person-other than a patient's representative acting on the patient's behalf-who receives information privileged under this rule may disclose the information only to the extent consistent with the purposes for which it was obtained.

(c) **Who May Claim**. The privilege may be claimed by:

    (1) the patient; or

    (2) the patient's representative on the patient's behalf.

The professional may claim the privilege on the patient's behalf-and is presumed to have authority to do so.

(d) **Exceptions**. This privilege does not apply:

    (1) Proceeding Against Professional. If the communication or record is relevant to a claim or defense in:

      (A) a proceeding the patient brings against a professional; or

      (B) a license revocation proceeding in which the patient is a complaining witness.

    (2) Written Waiver. If the patient or a person authorized to act on the patient's behalf waives the privilege in writing.

    (3) Action to Collect. In an action to collect a claim for mental or emotional health services rendered to the patient.

    (4) Communication Made in Court-Ordered Examination. To a communication the patient made to a professional during a court-ordered examination relating to the patient's mental or emotional condition or disorder if:

      (A) the patient made the communication after being informed that it would not be privileged;

      (B) the communication is offered to prove an issue involving the patient's mental or emotional health; and

    (C) the court imposes appropriate safeguards against unauthorized disclosure.
(5) Party Relies on Patient's Condition. If any party relies on the patient's physical, mental, or emotional condition as a part of the party's claim or defense and the communication or record is relevant to that condition.
(6) Abuse or Neglect of "Institution" Resident. In a proceeding regarding the abuse or neglect, or the cause of any abuse or neglect, of a resident of an "institution" as defined in Tex. Health & Safety Code § 242.002.

History: Added Feb. 25, 1998, eff. March 1, 1998; amended effective April 1, 2015.

Comment to 2015 Restyling: The mental-health-information privilege in civil cases was enacted in Texas in 1979. Tex. Rev. Civ. Stat. art. 5561h (later codified at Tex. Health & Safety Code § 611.001 et seq.) provided that the privilege applied even if the patient had received the professional's services before the statute's enactment. Because more than thirty years have now passed, it is no longer necessary to burden the text of the rule with a statement regarding the privilege's retroactive application. But deleting this statement from the rule's text is not intended as a substantive change in the law.

Tex. Health & Safety Code ch. 611 addresses confidentiality rules for communications between a patient and a mental-health professional and for the professional's treatment records. Many of these provisions apply in contexts other than court proceedings. Reconciling the provisions of Rule 510 with the parts of chapter 611 that address a mental-health-information privilege applicable to court proceedings is beyond the scope of the restyling project.

Rule 511. Waiver by Voluntary Disclosure

(a) **General Rule**. A person upon whom these rules confer a privilege against disclosure waives the privilege if:
    (1) the person or a predecessor of the person while holder of the privilege voluntarily discloses or consents to disclosure of any significant part of the privileged matter unless such disclosure itself is privileged; or

(2) the person or a representative of the person calls a person to whom privileged communications have been made to testify as to the person's character or character trait insofar as such communications are relevant to such character or character trait.

(b) **Lawyer-Client Privilege and Work Product; Limitations on Waiver**. Notwithstanding paragraph (a), the following provisions apply, in the circumstances set out, to disclosure of a communication or information covered by the lawyer-client privilege or work-product protection.

(1) *Disclosure Made in a Federal or State Proceeding or to a Federal or State Office or Agency; Scope of a Waiver*. When the disclosure is made in a federal proceeding or state proceeding of any state or to a federal office or agency or state office or agency of any state and waives the lawyer-client privilege or work-product protection, the waiver extends to an undisclosed communication or information only if:

(A) the waiver is intentional;

(B) the disclosed and undisclosed communications or information concern the same subject matter; and

(C) they ought in fairness to be considered together.

(2) *Inadvertent Disclosure in State Civil Proceedings*. When made in a Texas state proceeding, an inadvertent disclosure does not operate as a waiver if the holder followed the procedures of Rule of Civil Procedure 193.3(d).

(3) *Controlling Effect of a Court Order*. A disclosure made in litigation pending before a federal court or a state court of any state that has entered an order that the privilege or protection is not waived by disclosure connected with the litigation pending before that court is also not a waiver in a Texas state proceeding.

(4) *Controlling Effect of a Party Agreement*. An agreement on the effect of disclosure in a state proceeding of any state is binding only on the parties to the agreement, unless it is incorporated into a court order.

History: Added Feb. 25, 1998, eff. March 1, 1998; amended effective April 1, 2015.

Comment to 2015 Restyling: The amendments to Rule 511 are designed to align Texas law with federal law on waiver of privilege by voluntary disclosure. Subsection (a) sets forth the general rule. Subsection (b) incorporates the provisions of Federal Rule of Evidence 502. Like the federal rule, subsection (b) only addresses disclosure of communications or information covered by the lawyer-client privilege or work-product protection. These amendments do not affect the law governing waiver of other privileges or protections.

Rule 512. Privileged Matter Disclosed under Compulsion or Without Opportunity to Claim Privilege

A privilege claim is not defeated by a disclosure that was:
(a) compelled erroneously; or
(b) made without opportunity to claim the privilege.

History: Added Feb. 25, 1998, eff. March 1, 1998; amended effective April 1, 2015.

Rule 513. Comment On or Inference From a Privilege Claim; Instruction

(a) **Comment or Inference Not Permitted**. Except as permitted in Rule 504(b)(2), neither the court nor counsel may comment on a privilege claim-whether made in the present proceeding or previously-and the factfinder may not draw an inference from the claim.
(b) **Claiming Privilege Without the Jury's Knowledge**. To the extent practicable, the court must conduct a jury trial so that the making of a privilege claim is not suggested to the jury by any means.
(c) **Claim of Privilege Against Self-Incrimination in a Civil Case**. Subdivisions (a) and (b) do not apply to a party's claim, in the present civil case, of the privilege against self-incrimination.
(d) **Jury Instruction**. When this rule forbids a jury from drawing an inference from a privilege claim, the court must, on request of a party against whom the jury might draw the inference, instruct the jury accordingly.

History: Added Feb. 25, 1998, eff. March 1, 1998; amended effective April 1, 2015.

Article VI – Witnesses

Rule 601. Competency to Testify in General; "Dead Man's Rule"

(a) **In General**. Every person is competent to be a witness unless these rules provide otherwise. The following witnesses are incompetent:

    (1) *Insane Persons*. A person who is now insane or was insane at the time of the events about which the person is called to testify.

    (2) *Persons Lacking Sufficient Intellect*. A child-or any other person-whom the court examines and finds lacks sufficient intellect to testify concerning the matters in issue.

(b) **The "Dead Man's Rule."**

    (1) *Applicability*. The "Dead Man's Rule" applies only in a civil case:

        (A) by or against a party in the party's capacity as an executor, administrator, or guardian; or

        (B) by or against a decedent's heirs or legal representatives and based in whole or in part on the decedent's oral statement.

    (2) *General Rule*. In cases described in subparagraph (b)(1)(A), a party may not testify against another party about an oral statement by the testator, intestate, or ward. In cases described in subparagraph (b)(1)(B), a party may not testify against another party about an oral statement by the decedent.

    (3) *Exceptions*. A party may testify against another party about an oral statement by the testator, intestate, ward, or decedent if:

        (A) the party's testimony about the statement is corroborated; or

        (B) the opposing party calls the party to testify at the trial about the statement.

    (4) *Instructions*. If a court excludes evidence under paragraph (b)(2), the court must instruct the jury that the law prohibits a party from testifying about an oral statement by the testator, intestate, ward, or decedent unless the oral statement is corroborated or the opposing party calls the party to testify at the trial about the statement.

History: Added Feb. 25, 1998, eff. March 1, 1998; amended effective April 1, 2015.

Comment to 2015 Restyling: The text of the "Dead Man's Rule" has been streamlined to clarify its meaning without making any substantive changes. The text of former Rule 601(b) (as well as its statutory predecessor, Vernon's Ann. Civ. St. art. 3716) prohibits only a "party" from testifying about the dead man's statements. Despite this, the last sentence of former Rule 601(b) requires the court to instruct the jury when the rule "prohibits an interested party or witness" from testifying. Because the rule prohibits only a "party" from testifying, restyled Rule 601(b)(4) references only "a party," and not "an interested party or witness." To be sure, courts have indicated that the rule (or its statutory predecessor) may be applicable to a witness who is not nominally a party and inapplicable to a witness who is only nominally a party. *See, e.g., Chandler v. Welborn*, 156 Tex. 312, 294 S.W.2d 801, 809 (1956); *Ragsdale v. Ragsdale*, 142 Tex. 476, 179 S.W.2d 291, 295 (1944). But these decisions are based on an interpretation of the meaning of "party." Therefore, limiting the court's instruction under restyled Rule 601(b)(4) to "a party" does not change Texas practice. In addition, restyled Rule 601(b) deletes the sentence in former Rule 601(b) that states "[e]xcept for the foregoing, a witness is not precluded from giving evidence . . . because the witness is a party to the action . . . ." This sentence is surplusage. Rule 601(b) is a rule of exclusion. If the testimony falls outside the rule of exclusion, its admissibility will be determined by other applicable rules of evidence.

Rule 602. Need for Personal Knowledge

A witness may testify to a matter only if evidence is introduced sufficient to support a finding that the witness has personal knowledge of the matter. Evidence to prove personal knowledge may consist of the witness's own testimony. This rule does not apply to a witness's expert testimony under Rule 703.

History: Added Feb. 25, 1998, eff. March 1, 1998; amended effective April 1, 2015.

Rule 603. Oath or Affirmation to Testify Truthfully

Before testifying, a witness must give an oath or affirmation to testify truthfully. It must be in a form designed to impress that duty on the witness's conscience.

History: Added Feb. 25, 1998, eff. March 1, 1998; amended effective
April 1, 2015.

Rule 604. Interpreter

An interpreter must be qualified and must give an oath or affirmation to
make a true translation.
History: Added Feb. 25, 1998, eff. March 1, 1998; amended effective
April 1, 2015.

Rule 605. Judge's Competency as a Witness

The presiding judge may not testify as a witness at the trial. A party need
not object to preserve the issue.

History: Added Feb. 25, 1998, eff. March 1, 1998; amended effective
April 1, 2015.

Rule 606. Juror's Competency as a Witness

(a) **At the Trial**. A juror may not testify as a witness before the other
jurors at the trial. If a juror is called to testify, the court must give a
party an opportunity to object outside the jury's presence.
(b) **During an Inquiry into the Validity of a Verdict or Indictment**.
   (1) *Prohibited Testimony or Other Evidence*. During an inquiry into
   the validity of a verdict or indictment, a juror may not testify
   about any statement made or incident that occurred during the
   jury's deliberations; the effect of anything on that juror's or
   another juror's vote; or any juror's mental processes concerning
   the verdict or indictment. The court may not receive a juror's
   affidavit or evidence of a juror's statement on these matters.
   (2) *Exceptions*. A juror may testify:
      (A) about whether an outside influence was improperly brought
      to bear on any juror; or
      (B) to rebut a claim that the juror was not qualified to serve.

History: Added Feb. 25, 1998, eff. March 1, 1998; amended effective
April 1, 2015.

Rule 607. Who May Impeach a Witness

Any party, including the party that called the witness, may attack the witness's credibility.

History: Added Feb. 25, 1998, eff. March 1, 1998; amended effective April 1, 2015.

Rule 608. A Witness's Character for Truthfulness or Untruthfulness

(a) **Reputation or Opinion Evidence**. A witness's credibility may be attacked or supported by testimony about the witness's reputation for having a character for truthfulness or untruthfulness, or by testimony in the form of an opinion about that character. But evidence of truthful character is admissible only after the witness's character for truthfulness has been attacked.

(b) **Specific Instances of Conduct**. Except for a criminal conviction under Rule 609, a party may not inquire into or offer extrinsic evidence to prove specific instances of the witness's conduct in order to attack or support the witness's character for truthfulness.

History: Added Feb. 25, 1998, eff. March 1, 1998; amended effective April 1, 2015.

Rule 609. Impeachment by Evidence of a Criminal Conviction

(a) **In General**. Evidence of a criminal conviction offered to attack a witness's character for truthfulness must be admitted if:
    (1) the crime was a felony or involved moral turpitude, regardless of punishment;
    (2) the probative value of the evidence outweighs its prejudicial effect to a party; and
    (3) it is elicited from the witness or established by public record.

(b) **Limit on Using the Evidence After 10 Years**. This subdivision (b) applies if more than 10 years have passed since the witness's conviction or release from confinement for it, whichever is later. Evidence of the conviction is admissible only if its probative value, supported by specific facts and circumstances, substantially outweighs its prejudicial effect.

(c) **Effect of a Pardon, Annulment, or Certificate of Rehabilitation**. Evidence of a conviction is not admissible if:
   (1) the conviction has been the subject of a pardon, annulment, certificate of rehabilitation, or other equivalent procedure based on a finding that the person has been rehabilitated, and the person has not been convicted of a later crime that was classified as a felony or involved moral turpitude, regardless of punishment;
   (2) probation has been satisfactorily completed for the conviction, and the person has not been convicted of a later crime that was classified as a felony or involved moral turpitude, regardless of punishment; or
   (3) the conviction has been the subject of a pardon, annulment, or other equivalent procedure based on a finding of innocence.
(d) **Juvenile Adjudications**. Evidence of a juvenile adjudication is admissible under this rule only if:
   (1) the witness is a party in a proceeding conducted under title 3 of the Texas Family Code; or
   (2) the United States or Texas Constitution requires that it be admitted.
(e) **Pendency of an Appeal**. A conviction for which an appeal is pending is not admissible under this rule.
(f) **Notice**. Evidence of a witness's conviction is not admissible under this rule if, after receiving from the adverse party a timely written request specifying the witness, the proponent of the conviction fails to provide sufficient written notice of intent to use the conviction. Notice is sufficient if it provides a fair opportunity to contest the use of such evidence.

History: Added Feb. 25, 1998, eff. March 1, 1998; amended effective April 1, 2015.

Rule 610. Religious Beliefs or Opinions

Evidence of a witness's religious beliefs or opinions is not admissible to attack or support the witness's credibility.

History: Added Feb. 25, 1998, eff. March 1, 1998; amended effective April 1, 2015.

Rule 611. Mode and Order of Examining Witnesses and Presenting Evidence

(a) **Control by the Court; Purposes**. The court should exercise reasonable control over the mode and order of examining witnesses and presenting evidence so as to:
   (1) make those procedures effective for determining the truth;
   (2) avoid wasting time; and
   (3) protect witnesses from harassment or undue embarrassment.
(b) **Scope of Cross-Examination**. A witness may be cross-examined on any relevant matter, including credibility.
(c) **Leading Questions**. Leading questions should not be used on direct examination except as necessary to develop the witness's testimony. Ordinarily, the court should allow leading questions:
   (1) on cross-examination; and
   (2) when a party calls a hostile witness, an adverse party, or a witness identified with an adverse party.

History: Added Feb. 25, 1998, eff. March 1, 1998; amended effective April 1, 2015.

Rule 612. Writing Used to Refresh a Witness's Memory

(a) **Scope**. This rule gives an adverse party certain options when a witness uses a writing to refresh memory:
   (1) while testifying;
   (2) before testifying, in civil cases, if the court decides that justice requires the party to have those options; or
   (3) before testifying, in criminal cases.
(b) **Adverse Party's Options; Deleting Unrelated Matter**. An adverse party is entitled to have the writing produced at the hearing, to inspect it, to cross-examine the witness about it, and to introduce in evidence any portion that relates to the witness's testimony. If the producing party claims that the writing includes unrelated matter, the court must examine the writing in camera, delete any unrelated portion, and order that the rest be delivered to the adverse party. Any portion deleted over objection must be preserved for the record.
(c) **Failure to Produce or Deliver the Writing**. If a writing is not produced or is not delivered as ordered, the court may issue any appropriate order. But if the prosecution does not comply in a

criminal case, the court must strike the witness's testimony or-if justice so requires-declare a mistrial.

History: Added Feb. 25, 1998, eff. March 1, 1998; amended effective April 1, 2015.

Rule 613. Witness's Prior Statement and Bias or Interest

(a) **Witness's Prior Inconsistent Statement**.
    (1) *Foundation Requirement*. When examining a witness about the witness's prior inconsistent statement-whether oral or written-a party must first tell the witness:
        (A) the contents of the statement;
        (B) the time and place of the statement; and
        (C) the person to whom the witness made the statement.
    (2) *Need Not Show Written Statement*. If the witness's prior inconsistent statement is written, a party need not show it to the witness before inquiring about it, but must, upon request, show it to opposing counsel.
    (3) *Opportunity to Explain or Deny*. A witness must be given the opportunity to explain or deny the prior inconsistent statement.
    (4) *Extrinsic Evidence*. Extrinsic evidence of a witness's prior inconsistent statement is not admissible unless the witness is first examined about the statement and fails to unequivocally admit making the statement.
    (5) *Opposing Party's Statement*. This subdivision (a) does not apply to an opposing party's statement under Rule 801(e)(2).

(b) **Witness's Bias or Interest**.
    (1) *Foundation Requirement*. When examining a witness about the witness's bias or interest, a party must first tell the witness the circumstances or statements that tend to show the witness's bias or interest. If examining a witness about a statement-whether oral or written-to prove the witness's bias or interest, a party must tell the witness:
        (A) the contents of the statement;
        (B) the time and place of the statement; and
        (C) the person to whom the statement was made.
    (2) *Need Not Show Written Statement*. If a party uses a written statement to prove the witness's bias or interest, a party need not show the statement to the witness before inquiring about it, but must, upon request, show it to opposing counsel.

(3) *Opportunity to Explain or Deny*. A witness must be given the opportunity to explain or deny the circumstances or statements that tend to show the witness's bias or interest. And the witness's proponent may present evidence to rebut the charge of bias or interest.

(4) *Extrinsic Evidence*. Extrinsic evidence of a witness's bias or interest is not admissible unless the witness is first examined about the bias or interest and fails to unequivocally admit it.

(c) **Witness's Prior Consistent Statement**. Unless Rule 801(e)(1)(B) provides otherwise, a witness's prior consistent statement is not admissible if offered solely to enhance the witness's credibility.

History: Added Feb. 25, 1998, eff. March 1, 1998; amended effective April 1, 2015.

Comment to 2015 Restyling: The amended rule retains the requirement that a witness be given an opportunity to explain or deny (a) a prior inconsistent statement or (b) the circumstances or a statement showing the witness's bias or interest, but this requirement is not imposed on the examining attorney. A witness may have to wait until redirect examination to explain a prior inconsistent statement or the circumstances or a statement that shows bias. But the impeaching attorney still is not permitted to introduce extrinsic evidence of the witness's prior inconsistent statement or bias unless the witness has first been examined about the statement or bias and has failed to unequivocally admit it. All other changes to the rule are intended to be stylistic only.

Rule 614. Excluding Witnesses

At a party's request, the court must order witnesses excluded so that they cannot hear other witnesses' testimony. Or the court may do so on its own. But this rule does not authorize excluding:

(a) a party who is a natural person and, in civil cases, that person's spouse;

(b) after being designated as the party's representative by its attorney:

(1) in a civil case, an officer or employee of a party that is not a natural person; or

(2) in a criminal case, a defendant that is not a natural person;

(c) a person whose presence a party shows to be essential to presenting the party's claim or defense; or

(d) the victim in a criminal case, unless the court determines that the victim's testimony would be materially affected by hearing other testimony at the trial.

History: Added Feb. 25, 1998, eff. March 1, 1998; amended effective April 1, 2015.

Rule 615. Producing a Witness's Statement in Criminal Cases

(a) **Motion to Produce**. After a witness other than the defendant testifies on direct examination, the court, on motion of a party who did not call the witness, must order an attorney for the state or the defendant and the defendant's attorney to produce, for the examination and use of the moving party, any statement of the witness that:

    (1) is in their possession;

    (2) relates to the subject matter of the witness's testimony; and

    (3) has not previously been produced.

(b) **Producing the Entire Statement**. If the entire statement relates to the subject matter of the witness's testimony, the court must order that the statement be delivered to the moving party.

(c) **Producing a Redacted Statement**. If the party who called the witness claims that the statement contains information that does not relate to the subject matter of the witness's testimony, the court must inspect the statement in camera. After excising any unrelated portions, the court must order delivery of the redacted statement to the moving party. If a party objects to an excision, the court must preserve the entire statement with the excised portion indicated, under seal, as part of the record.

(d) **Recess to Examine a Statement**. If the court orders production of a witness's statement, the court, on request, must recess the proceedings to allow the moving party time to examine the statement and prepare for its use.

(e) **Sanction for Failure to Produce or Deliver a Statement**. If the party who called the witness disobeys an order to produce or deliver a statement, the court must strike the witness's testimony from the record. If an attorney for the state disobeys the order, the court must declare a mistrial if justice so requires.

(f) **"Statement" Defined**. As used in this rule, a witness's "statement" means:

(1) a written statement that the witness makes and signs, or otherwise adopts or approves;

(2) a substantially verbatim, contemporaneously recorded recital of the witness's oral statement that is contained in any recording or any transcription of a recording; or

(3) the witness's statement to a grand jury, however taken or recorded, or a transcription of such a statement.

History: Added Feb. 25, 1998, eff. March 1, 1998; amended effective April 1, 2015; last amended effective January 1, 2016.

Comment to 2015 Amendment: The Michael Morton Act, codified at Texas Code of Criminal Procedure art. 39.14, affords defendants substantial pre-trial discovery, requiring the state, upon request from the defendant, to produce and permit the defendant to inspect and copy various items, including witness statements. In many instances, therefore, art. 39.14 eliminates the need, after the witness testifies on direct examination, for a defendant to request, and the court to order, production of a witness's statement. But art. 39.14 does not entirely eliminate the need for in-trial discovery of witness statements. Art. 39.14 does not extend equivalent discovery rights to the prosecution, and so prosecutors will still need to use Rule 615 to obtain witness statements of defense witnesses. Moreover, some defendants may fail to exercise their discovery rights under art. 39.14 and so may wish to obtain a witness statement under Rule 615. In addition, the Michael Morton Act applies only to the prosecution of offenses committed after December 31, 2013. Defendants on trial for offenses committed before then have no right to pre-trial discovery of the witness statements of prosecution witnesses.

Consequently, Rule 615(a) has been amended to account for the changed pre-trial discovery regime introduced by the Michael Morton Act. If a party's adversary has already produced a witness's statement - whether through formal discovery under art. 39.14 or through more informal means - Rule 615(a) no longer gives a party the right to obtain, after the witness testifies on direct examination, a court order for production of the witness's statement. But if a party's adversary has not already produced a witness's statement, the party may still use Rule 615(a) to request and obtain a court order requiring production of the witness's statement after the witness finishes testifying on direct examination.

Article VII – Opinions and Expert Testimony

Rule 701. Opinion Testimony by Lay Witnesses

If a witness is not testifying as an expert, testimony in the form of an opinion is limited to one that is:

(a) rationally based on the witness's perception; and

(b) helpful to clearly understanding the witness's testimony or to determining a fact in issue.

History: Added Feb. 25, 1998, eff. March 1, 1998; amended effective April 1, 2015.

Comment to 2015 Restyling: All references to an "inference" have been deleted because this makes the Rule flow better and easier to read, and because any "inference" is covered by the broader term "opinion." Courts have not made substantive decisions on the basis of any distinction between an opinion and an inference. No change in current practice is intended.

Rule 702. Testimony by Expert Witnesses

A witness who is qualified as an expert by knowledge, skill, experience, training, or education may testify in the form of an opinion or otherwise if the expert's scientific, technical, or other specialized knowledge will help the trier of fact to understand the evidence or to determine a fact in issue.

History: Added Feb. 25, 1998, eff. March 1, 1998; amended effective April 1, 2015.

Rule 703. Bases of an Expert's Opinion Testimony

An expert may base an opinion on facts or data in the case that the expert has been made aware of, reviewed, or personally observed. If experts in the particular field would reasonably rely on those kinds of facts or data in forming an opinion on the subject, they need not be admissible for the opinion to be admitted.

History: Added Feb. 25, 1998, eff. March 1, 1998; amended effective April 1, 2015.

Comment to 2015 Restyling: All references to an "inference" have been deleted because this makes the Rule flow better and easier to read, and because any "inference" is covered by the broader term "opinion." Courts have not made substantive decisions on the basis of any distinction between an opinion and an inference. No change in current practice is intended.

Rule 704. Opinion on Ultimate Issue

An opinion is not objectionable just because it embraces an ultimate issue.

History: Added Feb. 25, 1998, eff. March 1, 1998; amended effective April 1, 2015.

Rule 705. Disclosing the Underlying Facts or Data and Examining an Expert About Them

(a) **Stating an Opinion Without Disclosing the Underlying Facts or Data**. Unless the court orders otherwise, an expert may state an opinion-and give the reasons for it-without first testifying to the underlying facts or data. But the expert may be required to disclose those facts or data on cross-examination.

(b) **Voir Dire Examination of an Expert About the Underlying Facts or Data**. Before an expert states an opinion or discloses the underlying facts or data, an adverse party in a civil case may-or in a criminal case must-be permitted to examine the expert about the underlying facts or data. This examination must take place outside the jury's hearing.

(c) **Admissibility of Opinion**. An expert's opinion is inadmissible if the underlying facts or data do not provide a sufficient basis for the opinion.

(d) **When Otherwise Inadmissible Underlying Facts or Data May Be Disclosed; Instructing the Jury**. If the underlying facts or data would otherwise be inadmissible, the proponent of the opinion may not disclose them to the jury if their probative value in helping the jury evaluate the opinion is outweighed by their prejudicial effect. If the court allows the proponent to disclose those facts or data the court must, upon timely request, restrict the evidence to its proper scope and instruct the jury accordingly.

History: Added Feb. 25, 1998, eff. March 1, 1998; amended effective April 1, 2015.

Comment to 2015 Restyling: All references to an "inference" have been deleted because this makes the Rule flow better and easier to read, and because any "inference" is covered by the broader term "opinion." Courts have not made substantive decisions on the basis of any distinction between an opinion and an inference. No change in current practice is intended.

Rule 706. Audit in Civil Cases

Notwithstanding any other evidence rule, the court must admit an auditor's verified report prepared under Rule of Civil Procedure 172 and offered by a party. If a party files exceptions to the report, a party may offer evidence supporting the exceptions to contradict the report.

History: Added Feb. 25, 1998, eff. March 1, 1998; amended effective April 1, 2015.

Article VIII – Hearsay

Rule 801. Definitions That Apply to This Article; Exclusions from Hearsay

(a) **Statement**. "Statement" means a person's oral or written verbal expression, or nonverbal conduct that a person intended as a substitute for verbal expression.
(b) **Declarant**. "Declarant" means the person who made the statement.
(c) **Matter Asserted**. "Matter asserted" means:
  (1) any matter a declarant explicitly asserts; and
  (2) any matter implied by a statement, if the probative value of the statement as offered flows from the declarant's belief about the matter.
(d) **Hearsay**. "Hearsay" means a statement that:
  (1) the declarant does not make while testifying at the current trial or hearing; and
  (2) a party offers in evidence to prove the truth of the matter asserted in the statement.

(e) **Statements That Are Not Hearsay**. A statement that meets the following conditions is not hearsay:

    (1) *A Declarant-Witness's Prior Statement*. The declarant testifies and is subject to cross-examination about a prior statement, and the statement:

        (A) is inconsistent with the declarant's testimony and:

            (i) when offered in a civil case, was given under penalty of perjury at a trial, hearing, or other proceeding or in a deposition; or

            (ii) when offered in a criminal case, was given under penalty of perjury at a trial, hearing, or other proceeding-except a grand jury proceeding-or in a deposition;

        (B) is consistent with the declarant's testimony and is offered to rebut an express or implied charge that the declarant recently fabricated it or acted from a recent improper influence or motive in so testifying; or

        (C) identifies a person as someone the declarant perceived earlier.

    (2) *An Opposing Party's Statement*. The statement is offered against an opposing party and:

        (A) was made by the party in an individual or representative capacity;

        (B) is one the party manifested that it adopted or believed to be true;

        (C) was made by a person whom the party authorized to make a statement on the subject;

        (D) was made by the party's agent or employee on a matter within the scope of that relationship and while it existed; or

        (E) was made by the party's coconspirator during and in furtherance of the conspiracy.

    (3) *A Deponent's Statement*. In a civil case, the statement was made in a deposition taken in the same proceeding. "Same proceeding" is defined in Rule of Civil Procedure 203.6(b). The deponent's unavailability as a witness is not a requirement for admissibility.

History: Added Feb. 25, 1998, eff. March 1, 1998; amended effective April 1, 2015.

Comment to 2015 Restyling: Statements falling under the hearsay exclusion provided by Rule 801(e)(2) are no longer referred to as "admissions" in the title to the subdivision. The term "admissions" is confusing because not all statements covered by the exclusion are admissions in the colloquial sense-a statement can be within the exclusion even if it "admitted" nothing and was not against the party's interest when made. The term "admissions" also raises confusion in comparison with the Rule 803(24) exception for declarations against interest. No change in application of the exclusion is intended.

The deletion of former Rule 801(e)(1)(D), which cross-references Code of Criminal Procedure art. 38.071, is not intended as a substantive change. Including this cross-reference made sense when the Texas Rules of Criminal Evidence were first promulgated, but with subsequent changes to the statutory provision, its inclusion is no longer appropriate. The version of article 38.071 that was initially cross-referenced in the Rules of Criminal Evidence required the declarant-victim to be available to testify at the trial. That requirement has since been deleted from the statute, and the statute no longer requires either the availability or testimony of the declarant-victim. Thus, cross-referencing the statute in Rule 801(e)(1), which applies only when the declarant testifies at trial about the prior statement, no longer makes sense. Moreover, article 38.071 is but one of a number of statutes that mandate the admission of certain hearsay statements in particular circumstances. See, e.g., Code of Criminal Procedure art. 38.072; Family Code §§ 54.031, 104.002, 104.006. These statutory provisions take precedence over the general rule excluding hearsay, see Rules 101(c) and 802, and there is no apparent justification for cross-referencing article 38.071 and not all other such provisions.

Rule 802. The Rule Against Hearsay

Hearsay is not admissible unless any of the following provides otherwise:
- a statute;
- these rules; or
- other rules prescribed under statutory authority.

Inadmissible hearsay admitted without objection may not be denied probative value merely because it is hearsay.

History: Added Feb. 25, 1998, eff. March 1, 1998; amended effective April 1, 2015.

Rule 803. Exceptions to the Rule Against Hearsay-Regardless of Whether the Declarant Is Available as a Witness

The following are not excluded by the rule against hearsay, regardless of whether the declarant is available as a witness:

(1) **Present Sense Impression**. A statement describing or explaining an event or condition, made while or immediately after the declarant perceived it.

(2) **Excited Utterance**. A statement relating to a startling event or condition, made while the declarant was under the stress of excitement that it caused.

(3) **Then-Existing Mental, Emotional, or Physical Condition**. A statement of the declarant's then-existing state of mind (such as motive, intent, or plan) or emotional, sensory, or physical condition (such as mental feeling, pain, or bodily health), but not including a statement of memory or belief to prove the fact remembered or believed unless it relates to the validity or terms of the declarant's will.

(4) **Statement Made for Medical Diagnosis or Treatment**. A statement that:
    (A) is made for-and is reasonably pertinent to-medical diagnosis or treatment; and
    (B) describes medical history; past or present symptoms or sensations; their inception; or their general cause.

(5) **Recorded Recollection**. A record that:
    (A) is on a matter the witness once knew about but now cannot recall well enough to testify fully and accurately;
    (B) was made or adopted by the witness when the matter was fresh in the witness's memory; and
    (C) accurately reflects the witness's knowledge, unless the circumstances of the record's preparation cast doubt on its trustworthiness.
If admitted, the record may be read into evidence but may be received as an exhibit only if offered by an adverse party.

(6) **Records of a Regularly Conducted Activity**. A record of an act, event, condition, opinion, or diagnosis if:

(A) the record was made at or near the time by-or from information transmitted by-someone with knowledge;

(B) the record was kept in the course of a regularly conducted business activity;

(C) making the record was a regular practice of that activity;

(D) all these conditions are shown by the testimony of the custodian or another qualified witness, or by an affidavit or unsworn declaration that complies with Rule 902(10); and

(E) the opponent fails to demonstrate that the source of information or the method or circumstances of preparation indicate a lack of trustworthiness.

"Business" as used in this paragraph includes every kind of regular organized activity whether conducted for profit or not.

(7) **Absence of a Record of a Regularly Conducted Activity**. Evidence that a matter is not included in a record described in paragraph (6) if:

(A) the evidence is admitted to prove that the matter did not occur or exist;

(B) a record was regularly kept for a matter of that kind; and

(C) the opponent fails to show that the possible source of the information or other circumstances indicate a lack of trustworthiness.

(8) **Public Records**. A record or statement of a public office if:

(A) it sets out:

(i) the office's activities;

(ii) a matter observed while under a legal duty to report, but not including, in a criminal case, a matter observed by law-enforcement personnel; or

(iii) in a civil case or against the government in a criminal case, factual findings from a legally authorized investigation; and

(B) the opponent fails to demonstrate that the source of information or other circumstances indicate a lack of trustworthiness.

(9) **Public Records of Vital Statistics**. A record of a birth, death, or marriage, if reported to a public office in accordance with a legal duty.

(10)**Absence of a Public Record**. Testimony-or a certification under Rule 902-that a diligent search failed to disclose a public record or statement if the testimony or certification is admitted to prove that:

    (A) the record or statement does not exist; or

    (B) a matter did not occur or exist, if a public office regularly kept a record or statement for a matter of that kind.

(11) **Records of Religious Organizations Concerning Personal or Family History**. A statement of birth, legitimacy, ancestry, marriage, divorce, death, relationship by blood or marriage, or similar facts of personal or family history, contained in a regularly kept record of a religious organization.

(12) **Certificates of Marriage, Baptism, and Similar Ceremonies**. A statement of fact contained in a certificate:

    (A) made by a person who is authorized by a religious organization or by law to perform the act certified;

    (B) attesting that the person performed a marriage or similar ceremony or administered a sacrament; and

    (C) purporting to have been issued at the time of the act or within a reasonable time after it.

(13) **Family Records**. A statement of fact about personal or family history contained in a family record, such as a Bible, genealogy, chart, engraving on a ring, inscription on a portrait, or engraving on an urn or burial marker.

(14) **Records of Documents That Affect an Interest in Property**. The record of a document that purports to establish or affect an interest in property if:

    (A) the record is admitted to prove the content of the original recorded document, along with its signing and its delivery by each person who purports to have signed it;

    (B) the record is kept in a public office; and

    (C) a statute authorizes recording documents of that kind in that office.

(15) **Statements in Documents That Affect an Interest in Property**. A statement contained in a document that purports to establish or affect an interest in property if the matter stated was relevant to the document's purpose-unless later dealings with the property are inconsistent with the truth of the statement or the purport of the document.

(16) **Statements in Ancient Documents**. A statement in a document that is at least 20 years old and whose authenticity is established.

(17) **Market Reports and Similar Commercial Publications**.
Market quotations, lists, directories, or other compilations that
are generally relied on by the public or by persons in particular
occupations.

(18) **Statements in Learned Treatises, Periodicals, or Pamphlets**.
A statement contained in a treatise, periodical, or pamphlet if:

(A) the statement is called to the attention of an expert witness
on cross-examination or relied on by the expert on direct
examination; and

(B) the publication is established as a reliable authority by the
expert's admission or testimony, by another expert's
testimony, or by judicial notice.

If admitted, the statement may be read into evidence but not
received as an exhibit.

(19) **Reputation Concerning Personal or Family History**. A
reputation among a person's family by blood, adoption, or
marriage-or among a person's associates or in the community-
concerning the person's birth, adoption, legitimacy, ancestry,
marriage, divorce, death, relationship by blood, adoption, or
marriage, or similar facts of personal or family History:

(20) **Reputation Concerning Boundaries or General History**. A
reputation in a community-arising before the controversy-
concerning boundaries of land in the community or customs that
affect the land, or concerning general historical events important
to that community, state, or nation.

(21) **Reputation Concerning Character**. A reputation among a
person's associates or in the community concerning the person's
character.

(22) **Judgment of a Previous Conviction**. Evidence of a final
judgment of conviction if:

(A) it is offered in a civil case and:

(i) the judgment was entered after a trial or guilty plea, but
not a nolo contendere plea;

(ii) the conviction was for a felony;

(iii) the evidence is admitted to prove any fact essential to
the judgment; and

(iv) an appeal of the conviction is not pending; or

(B) it is offered in a criminal case and:

(i) the judgment was entered after a trial or a guilty or
nolo contendere plea;

     (ii) the conviction was for a criminal offense;

     (iii) the evidence is admitted to prove any fact essential to the judgment;

     (iv) when offered by the prosecutor for a purpose other than impeachment, the judgment was against the defendant; and

     (v) an appeal of the conviction is not pending.

(23) **Judgments Involving Personal, Family, or General History or a Boundary**. A judgment that is admitted to prove a matter of personal, family, or general history, or boundaries, if the matter:

    (A) was essential to the judgment; and

    (B) could be proved by evidence of reputation.

(24) **Statement Against Interest**. A statement that:

    (A) a reasonable person in the declarant's position would have made only if the person believed it to be true because, when made, it was so contrary to the declarant's proprietary or pecuniary interest or had so great a tendency to invalidate the declarant's claim against someone else or to expose the declarant to civil or criminal liability or to make the declarant an object of hatred, ridicule, or disgrace; and

    (B) is supported by corroborating circumstances that clearly indicate its trustworthiness, if it is offered in a criminal case as one that tends to expose the declarant to criminal liability.

History: Added Feb. 25, 1998, eff. March 1, 1998; amended effective April 1, 2015.

Rule 804. Exceptions to the Rule Against Hearsay-When the Declarant Is Unavailable as a Witness

(a) **Criteria for Being Unavailable**. A declarant is considered to be unavailable as a witness if the declarant:

    (1) is exempted from testifying about the subject matter of the declarant's statement because the court rules that a privilege applies;

    (2) refuses to testify about the subject matter despite a court order to do so;

    (3) testifies to not remembering the subject matter;

(4) cannot be present or testify at the trial or hearing because of death or a then-existing infirmity, physical illness, or mental illness; or

(5) is absent from the trial or hearing and the statement's proponent has not been able, by process or other reasonable means, to procure the declarant's attendance or testimony. But this subdivision (a) does not apply if the statement's proponent procured or wrongfully caused the declarant's unavailability as a witness in order to prevent the declarant from attending or testifying.

(b) **The Exceptions**. The following are not excluded by the rule against hearsay if the declarant is unavailable as a witness:

(1) *Former Testimony*. Testimony that:

(A) when offered in a civil case:

(i) was given as a witness at a trial or hearing of the current or a different proceeding or in a deposition in a different proceeding; and

(ii) is now offered against a party and the party-or a person with similar interest-had an opportunity and similar motive to develop the testimony by direct, cross-, or redirect examination.

(B) when offered in a criminal case:

(i) was given as a witness at a trial or hearing of the current or a different proceeding; and

(ii) is now offered against a party who had an opportunity and similar motive to develop it by direct, cross-, or redirect examination; or

(iii) was taken in a deposition under-and is now offered in accordance with-chapter 39 of the Code of Criminal Procedure.

(2) *Statement Under the Belief of Imminent Death*. A statement that the declarant, while believing the declarant's death to be imminent, made about its cause or circumstances.

(3) *Statement of Personal or Family History*. A statement about:

(A) the declarant's own birth, adoption, legitimacy, ancestry, marriage, divorce, relationship by blood, adoption or marriage, or similar facts of personal or family history, even though the declarant had no way of acquiring personal knowledge about that fact; or

(B) another person concerning any of these facts, as well as death, if the declarant was related to the person by blood, adoption, or marriage or was so intimately associated with the person's family that the declarant's information is likely to be accurate.

History: Added Feb. 25, 1998, eff. March 1, 1998; amended effective April 1, 2015.

Rule 805. Hearsay within Hearsay

Hearsay within hearsay is not excluded by the rule against hearsay if each part of the combined statements conforms with an exception to the rule.

History: Added Feb. 25, 1998, eff. March 1, 1998; amended effective April 1, 2015.

Rule 806. Attacking and Supporting the Declarant's Credibility

When a hearsay statement-or a statement described in Rule 801(e)(2)(C), (D), or (E), or, in a civil case, a statement described in Rule 801(e)(3)-has been admitted in evidence, the declarant's credibility may be attacked, and then supported, by any evidence that would be admissible for those purposes if the declarant had testified as a witness. The court may admit evidence of the declarant's statement or conduct, offered to impeach the declarant, regardless of when it occurred or whether the declarant had an opportunity to explain or deny it. If the party against whom the statement was admitted calls the declarant as a witness, the party may examine the declarant on the statement as if on cross-examination.

History: Added Feb. 25, 1998, eff. March 1, 1998; amended effective April 1, 2015.

Article IX – Authentication and Identification

Rule 901. Authenticating or Identifying Evidence

(a) **In General**. To satisfy the requirement of authenticating or identifying an item of evidence, the proponent must produce evidence sufficient to support a finding that the item is what the proponent claims it is.

(b) **Examples**. The following are examples only-not a complete list-of evidence that satisfies the requirement:

(1) *Testimony of a Witness with Knowledge*. Testimony that an item is what it is claimed to be.

(2) *Nonexpert Opinion About Handwriting*. A nonexpert's opinion that handwriting is genuine, based on a familiarity with it that was not acquired for the current litigation.

(3) *Comparison by an Expert Witness or the Trier of Fact*. A comparison by an expert witness or the trier of fact with a specimen that the court has found is genuine.

(4) *Distinctive Characteristics and the Like*. The appearance, contents, substance, internal patterns, or other distinctive characteristics of the item, taken together with all the circumstances.

(5) *Opinion About a Voice*. An opinion identifying a person's voice-whether heard firsthand or through mechanical or electronic transmission or recording-based on hearing the voice at any time under circumstances that connect it with the alleged speaker.

(6) *Evidence About a Telephone Conversation*. For a telephone conversation, evidence that a call was made to the number assigned at the time to:

(A) a particular person, if circumstances, including self-identification, show that the person answering was the one called; or

(B) a particular business, if the call was made to a business and the call related to business reasonably transacted over the telephone.

(7) *Evidence About Public Records*. Evidence that:

(A) a document was recorded or filed in a public office as authorized by law; or

(B) a purported public record or statement is from the office where items of this kind are kept.

(8) *Evidence About Ancient Documents or Data Compilations*. For a document or data compilation, evidence that it:

(A) is in a condition that creates no suspicion about its authenticity;

(B) was in a place where, if authentic, it would likely be; and

(C) is at least 20 years old when offered.

(9) *Evidence About a Process or System.* Evidence describing a process or system and showing that it produces an accurate result.

(10) *Methods Provided by a Statute or Rule.* Any method of authentication or identification allowed by a statute or other rule prescribed under statutory authority.

History: Added Feb. 25, 1998, eff. March 1, 1998; amended effective April 1, 2015.

Rule 902. Self-Authentication [Effective September 1, 2014]

The following items of evidence are self-authenticating; they require no extrinsic evidence of authenticity in order to be admitted:

(1) **Domestic Public Documents That Are Sealed and Signed.** A document that bears:

(A) a seal purporting to be that of the United States; any state, district, commonwealth, territory, or insular possession of the United States; the former Panama Canal Zone; the Trust Territory of the Pacific Islands; a political subdivision of any of these entities; or a department, agency, or officer of any entity named above; and

(B) a signature purporting to be an execution or attestation.

(2) **Domestic Public Documents That Are Not Sealed But Are Signed and Certified.** A document that bears no seal if:

(A) it bears the signature of an officer or employee of an entity named in Rule 902(1)(A); and

(B) another public officer who has a seal and official duties within that same entity certifies under seal-or its equivalent-that the signer has the official capacity and that the signature is genuine.

(3) **Foreign Public Documents.** A document that purports to be signed or attested by a person who is authorized by a foreign country's law to do so.

(A) In General. The document must be accompanied by a final certification that certifies the genuineness of the signature and official position of the signer or attester-or of any foreign official whose certificate of genuineness relates to the signature or attestation or is in a chain of certificates of genuineness relating to the signature or attestation. The certification may be made by a secretary of a United States embassy or legation; by a consul general, vice consul, or consular agent of the United States; or by a diplomatic or consular official of the foreign country assigned or accredited to the United States.

(B) If Parties Have Reasonable Opportunity to Investigate. If all parties have been given a reasonable opportunity to investigate the document's authenticity and accuracy, the court may, for good cause, either:

    (i) order that it be treated as presumptively authentic without final certification; or

    (ii) allow it to be evidenced by an attested summary with or without final certification.

(C) If a Treaty Abolishes or Displaces the Final Certification Requirement. If the United States and the foreign country in which the official record is located are parties to a treaty or convention that abolishes or displaces the final certification requirement, the record and attestation must be certified under the terms of the treaty or convention.

(4) **Certified Copies of Public Records**. A copy of an official record-or a copy of a document that was recorded or filed in a public office as authorized by law-if the copy is certified as correct by:

(A) the custodian or another person authorized to make the certification; or

(B) a certificate that complies with Rule 902(1), (2), or (3), a statute, or a rule prescribed under statutory authority.

(5) **Official Publications**. A book, pamphlet, or other publication purporting to be issued by a public authority.

(6) **Newspapers and Periodicals**. Printed material purporting to be a newspaper or periodical.

(7) **Trade Inscriptions and the Like**. An inscription, sign, tag, or label purporting to have been affixed in the course of business and indicating origin, ownership, or control.

(8) **Acknowledged Documents**. A document accompanied by a certificate of acknowledgment that is lawfully executed by a notary public or another officer who is authorized to take acknowledgments.

(9) **Commercial Paper and Related Documents**. Commercial paper, a signature on it, and related documents, to the extent allowed by general commercial law.

(10) **Business Records Accompanied by Affidavit**. The original or a copy of a record that meets the requirements of Rule 803(6) or (7), if the record is accompanied by an affidavit that complies with subparagraph (B) of this rule and any other requirements of law, and the record and affidavit are served in accordance with subparagraph (A). For good cause shown, the court may order that a business record be treated as presumptively authentic even if the proponent fails to comply with subparagraph (A).

(A) Service Requirement. The proponent of a record must serve the record and the accompanying affidavit on each other party to the case at least 14 days before trial. The record and affidavit may be served by any method permitted by Rule of Civil Procedure 21a.

(B) Form of Affidavit. An affidavit is sufficient if it includes the following language, but this form is not exclusive. The proponent may use an unsworn declaration made under penalty of perjury in place of an affidavit.

> 1. I am the custodian of records [or I am an employee or owner] of _____ and am familiar with the manner in which its records are created and maintained by virtue of my duties and responsibilities.
> 2. Attached are _____ pages of records. These are the original records or exact duplicates of the original records.
> 3. The records were made at or near the time of each act, event, condition, opinion, or diagnosis set forth. [or It is the regular practice of _____ to make this type of record at or near the time of each act, event, condition, opinion, or diagnosis set forth in the record.]
> 4. The records were made by, or from information transmitted by, persons with knowledge of the matters set forth. [or It is the regular practice of _____ for this type of record to be made by, or from information transmitted by, persons with knowledge of the matters set forth in them.]
> 5. The records were kept in the course of regularly conducted business activity. [or It is the regular

practice of _____ to keep this type of record in the course of regularly conducted business activity.]
6. It is the regular practice of the business activity to make the records.

(11)**Presumptions Under a Statute or Rule**. A signature, document, or anything else that a statute or rule prescribed under statutory authority declares to be presumptively or prima facie genuine or authentic.

History: Added Feb. 25, 1998, eff. March 1, 1998; amended November 13, 2012, effective March 1, 2013; amended April 14, 2014, effective September 1, 2014; amended effective April 1, 2015.

Rule 903. Subscribing Witness's Testimony

A subscribing witness's testimony is necessary to authenticate a writing only if required by the law of the jurisdiction that governs its validity.

History: Added Feb. 25, 1998, eff. March 1, 1998; amended effective April 1, 2015.

Article X – Contents of Writings, Recordings, and Photographs

Rule 1001. Definitions That Apply to This Article

In this article:
(a) A "writing" consists of letters, words, numbers, or their equivalent set down in any form.
(b) A "recording" consists of letters, words, numbers, or their equivalent recorded in any manner.
(c) A "photograph" means a photographic image or its equivalent stored in any form.
(d) An "original" of a writing or recording means the writing or recording itself or any counterpart intended to have the same effect by the person who executed or issued it. For electronically stored information, "original" means any printout-or other output readable by sight-if it accurately reflects the information. An "original" of a photograph includes the negative or a print from it.

(e) A "duplicate" means a counterpart produced by a mechanical, photographic, chemical, electronic, or other equivalent process or technique that accurately reproduces the original.

History: Added Feb. 25, 1998, eff. March 1, 1998; amended effective April 1, 2015.

Rule 1002. Requirement of the Original

An original writing, recording, or photograph is required in order to prove its content unless these rules or other law provides otherwise.

History: Added Feb. 25, 1998, eff. March 1, 1998; amended effective April 1, 2015.

Rule 1003. Admissibility of Duplicates

A duplicate is admissible to the same extent as the original unless a question is raised about the original's authenticity or the circumstances make it unfair to admit the duplicate.

History: Added Feb. 25, 1998, eff. March 1, 1998; amended effective April 1, 2015.

Rule 1004. Admissibility of Other Evidence of Content

An original is not required and other evidence of the content of a writing, recording, or photograph is admissible if:
(a) all the originals are lost or destroyed, unless the proponent lost or destroyed them in bad faith;
(b) an original cannot be obtained by any available judicial process;
(c) an original is not located in Texas;
(d) the party against whom the original would be offered had control of the original; was at that time put on notice, by pleadings or otherwise, that the original would be a subject of proof at the trial or hearing; and fails to produce it at the trial or hearing; or
(e) the writing, recording, or photograph is not closely related to a controlling issue.

History: Added Feb. 25, 1998, eff. March 1, 1998; amended effective April 1, 2015.

Rule 1005. Copies of Public Records to Prove Content

The proponent may use a copy to prove the content of an official record-or of a document that was recorded or filed in a public office as authorized by law-if these conditions are met: the record or document is otherwise admissible; and the copy is certified as correct in accordance with Rule 902(4) or is testified to be correct by a witness who has compared it with the original. If no such copy can be obtained by reasonable diligence, then the proponent may use other evidence to prove the content.

History: Added Feb. 25, 1998, eff. March 1, 1998; amended effective April 1, 2015.

Rule 1006. Summaries to Prove Content

The proponent may use a summary, chart, or calculation to prove the content of voluminous writings, recordings, or photographs that cannot be conveniently examined in court. The proponent must make the originals or duplicates available for examination or copying, or both, by other parties at a reasonable time and place. And the court may order the proponent to produce them in court.

History: Added Feb. 25, 1998, eff. March 1, 1998; amended effective April 1, 2015.

Rule 1007. Testimony or Statement of a Party to Prove Content

The proponent may prove the content of a writing, recording, or photograph by the testimony, deposition, or written statement of the party against whom the evidence is offered. The proponent need not account for the original.

History: Added Feb. 25, 1998, eff. March 1, 1998; amended effective April 1, 2015.

Rule 1008. Functions of the Court and Jury

Ordinarily, the court determines whether the proponent has fulfilled the factual conditions for admitting other evidence of the content of a writing, recording, or photograph under Rule 1004 or 1005. But in a jury trial, the jury determines-in accordance with Rule 104(b)-any issue about whether:

(a) an asserted writing, recording, or photograph ever existed;

(b) another one produced at the trial or hearing is the original; or

(c) other evidence of content accurately reflects the content.

History: Added Feb. 25, 1998, eff. March 1, 1998; amended effective April 1, 2015.

Rule 1009. Translating a Foreign Language Document

(a) **Submitting a Translation**. A translation of a foreign language document is admissible if, at least 45 days before trial, the proponent serves on all parties:

    (1) the translation and the underlying foreign language document; and

    (2) a qualified translator's affidavit or unsworn declaration that sets forth the translator's qualifications and certifies that the translation is accurate.

(b) **Objection**. When objecting to a translation's accuracy, a party should specifically indicate its inaccuracies and offer an accurate translation. A party must serve the objection on all parties at least 15 days before trial.

(c) **Effect of Failing to Object or Submit a Conflicting Translation**. If the underlying foreign language document is otherwise admissible, the court must admit-and may not allow a party to attack the accuracy of-a translation submitted under subdivision (a) unless the party has:

    (1) submitted a conflicting translation under subdivision (a); or

    (2) objected to the translation under subdivision (b).

(d) **Effect of Objecting or Submitting a Conflicting Translation**. If conflicting translations are submitted under subdivision (a) or an objection is made under subdivision (b), the court must determine whether there is a genuine issue about the accuracy of a material part of the translation. If so, the trier of fact must resolve the issue.

(e) **Qualified Translator May Testify**. Except for subdivision (c), this rule does not preclude a party from offering the testimony of a qualified translator to translate a foreign language document.

(f) **Time Limits**. On a party's motion and for good cause, the court may alter this rule's time limits.

(g) **Court-Appointed Translator**. If necessary, the court may appoint a qualified translator. The reasonable value of the translator's services must be taxed as court costs.

History: Added Feb. 25, 1998, eff. March 1, 1998; amended effective April 1, 2015.